DRAWING
MANGA MEN

ANNA SOUTHGATE AND YISHAN LI

rosen publishing's
rosen central

NEW YORK

This edition published in 2013 by:

The Rosen Publishing Group, Inc.
29 East 21st Street
New York, NY 10010

Library of Congress Cataloging-in-Publication Data

Southgate, Anna.
Drawing manga men/Anna Southgate, Yishan Li.—First [edition].
    pages cm.—(Teen guide to drawing manga)
Includes bibliographical references and index.
ISBN 978-1-4488-9240-2 (library binding)—
ISBN 978-1-4488-9261-7 (pbk.)—
ISBN 978-1-4488-9262-4 (6-pack)
1. Men in art—Juvenile literature. 2. Comic books, strips, etc.—Japan—Technique—Juvenile literature. 3. Cartooning—Technique—Juvenile literature. I. Li, Yishan. II. Li, Yishan. III. Title.
NC1764.8.M44S68 2013
741.5'1—dc23
                                      2012034784

Manufactured in the United States of America

CPSIA Compliance Information: Batch #W13YA: For further information, contact Rosen Publishing, New York, New York, at 1-800-237-9932.

All other content copyright © 2011 Axis Books Limited, London.

CONTENTS

INTRODUCTION

Manga—the term for Japanese-style comics—has become insanely popular all over the world. Fans of this art form typically want to read all the manga they can get their hands on. Inspired, many also want to create characters and stories of their own. If you would like to get started in creating your own manga, especially action-packed stories featuring male characters, this book will help you learn the basic art techniques and supplies you will need.

Male characters are featured in all kinds of manga, especially *shonen*, or boys' manga, which is full of nonstop action and humor. Drawing male manga characters can be exciting. Your manga men can be anything you want, including samurai warriors, ninjas, rock stars, gangsters, or the members of a future space crew. In addition, male manga characters are usually complex, and they don't always do what you might expect. Villains might change their ways for the better, and heroes might display negative traits or even commit terrible acts.

Manga characters, both male and female, have their own unique style that sets them apart from characters in other comics. First, the characters usually have large, exaggerated eyes and small mouths. With their large eyes, manga men and women can express a wide range of feelings, from friendliness and cheerfulness to burning anger. Slightly smaller eyes can be used to show coldness or hostility in a villain. Extreme displays of emotion are common in manga. Manga artists even use symbols to help communicate characters' emotions, such as large drops of sweat to show embarrassment. Sound effects are communicated visually, too, and dramatic poses and speed lines portray action.

If you would like to learn to draw your own manga, this book is a terrific place to start. The following pages explain top techniques for drawing male characters, including step-by-step instructions for drawing male faces, hair, bodies, and clothing. Practice these techniques, and before long you will be drawing manga men that pop right off the page.

There are several ways to produce manga art. You can draw and colour images by hand, generate them on a computer or work using a combination of both. Whichever style suits you, there are plenty of options when it comes to buying materials. This section of the book outlines the basics in terms of paper, pencils, inking pens, markers and paints, and will help you to make choices that work for you.

Artists have their preferences when it comes to equipment, but regardless of personal favourites, you will need a basic set of materials that will enable you to sketch, ink and colour your manga art. The items discussed here are only a guide – don't be afraid to experiment to find out what works best for you.

PAPERS

You will need two types of paper – one for creating sketches, the other for producing finished colour artwork.

For quickly jotting down ideas, almost any piece of scrap paper will do. For more developed sketching, though, use tracing paper. Tracing paper provides a smooth surface, helping you to sketch freely. It is also forgiving – any mistakes can easily be erased several times over. Typically, tracing paper comes in pads. Choose a pad that is around 90gsm (24lb) in weight for best results – lighter tracing papers may buckle and heavier ones are not suitable for sketching. Once you have finished sketching out ideas, you will need to transfer them to the paper you want to produce your finished coloured art on. To do this, you will have to trace over your pencil sketch, so the paper you choose cannot be too opaque or heavy – otherwise you will not be able to see the sketch underneath. Choose a paper around 60gsm (16lb) for this. The type of paper you use is also important. If you are going to colour using marker pens, use marker or layout paper. Both of these types are very good at holding the ink found in markers. Other papers of the same weight can cause the marker ink to bleed, that is, the ink soaks beyond the inked lines of your drawing and produces fuzzy edges. This does not look good. You may wish to colour your art using other materials, such as coloured pencils or watercolours. Drawing paper is good for graphite pencil and inked-only art (such as that found in the majority of manga comic books),

Experiment with different papers to find the one that suits your style of drawing and colouring best. Watercolour papers can be ideal if you like using lots of wet colour like inks to render your manga.

while heavyweight watercolour papers hold wet paint and coloured inks and come in a variety of surface textures.

Again, don't be afraid to experiment: you can buy many types of papers in single sheets while you find the ones that suit your artwork best.

PENCILS

The next step is to choose some pencils for your sketches. Pencil sketching is probably the most important stage, and always comes first when producing manga art (you cannot skip ahead to the inking stage), so make sure you choose pencils that feel good in your hand and allow you to express your ideas freely.

Pencils are manufactured in a range of hard and soft leads. Hard leads are designated by the letter H and soft leads by the letter B. Both come in six levels – 6H is the hardest lead and 6B is the softest. In the middle is HB, a halfway mark between the two ranges. Generally, an HB and a 2B lead will serve most sketching purposes, with the softer lead being especially useful for loose, idea sketches, and the harder for more final lines.

Alternatively, you can opt for mechanical pencils. Also called self-propelling pencils, these come in a variety of lead grades and widths and never lose their point, making sharpening traditional wood-cased pencils a thing of the past. Whether you use one is entirely up to you

Graphite pencils are ideal for getting your ideas down on paper, and producing your initial drawing. The pencil drawing is probably the most important stage in creating your artwork. Choose an HB and a 2B to start with.

– it is possible to get excellent results whichever model you choose.

COLOURED PENCILS

Coloured pencils are effective and versatile colouring tools. A good box of pencils contains around 100 colours and will last for a long time, since a blunt pencil just needs sharpening, not replacing or refilling. Unlike with markers, successive layers of tone and shade can be built up with the same pencil, by gradually increasing the pressure on the pencil lead.

COPIC MARKERS
WARM AND COOL GREYS

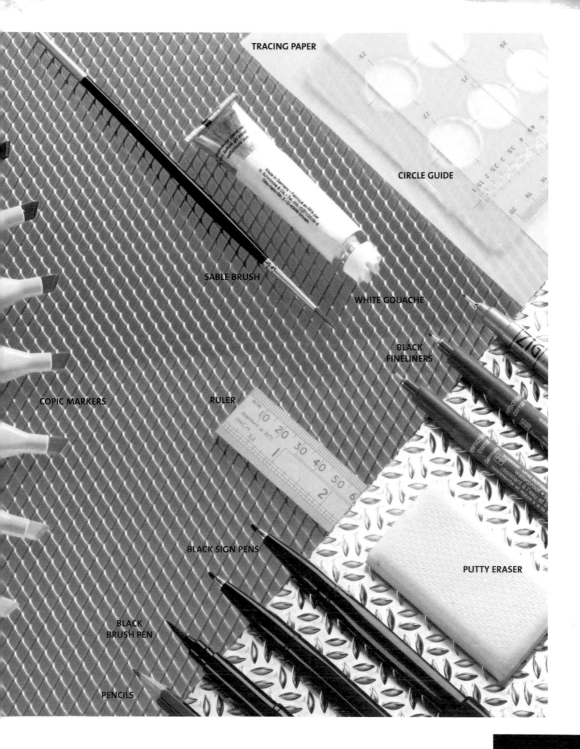

TRACING PAPER

CIRCLE GUIDE

SABLE BRUSH

WHITE GOUACHE

BLACK
FINELINERS

COPIC MARKERS

RULER

BLACK SIGN PENS

PUTTY ERASER

BLACK
BRUSH PEN

PENCILS

You can then build further colour by using a different colour pencil. Coloured pencils are also useful for adding detail, which is usually achieved by inking. This means that a more subtle level of detail can be achieved without having to ink in all lines. It is worth buying quality pencils. They do make a difference to the standard of your art and will not fade with age.

A good quality eraser or putty eraser is an essential item for removing unwanted pencil lines and for cleaning up your inked drawing before you start applying the colour.

SHARPENERS AND ERASERS

If you use wooden pencils, you will need to get a quality sharpener; this is a small but essential piece of equipment. Electric sharpeners work very well and are also very fast; they last a long time too. Otherwise, a handheld sharpener is fine. One that comes with a couple of spare blades can be a worthwhile investment, to ensure that your pencils are always sharp. Along with a sharpener, you will need an eraser

Felt-tip pens are the ideal way to ink your sketches. A fineliner, medium-tip pen and sign pen should meet all of your needs, whatever your style and preferred subjects. A few coloured felt-tip pens can be a good addition to your kit, allowing you to introduce colour at the inking stage.

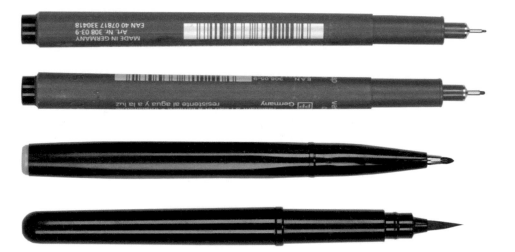

for removing any visible pencil lines from your inked sketches prior to colouring. Choose a high-quality eraser that does not smudge the pencil lead, scuff the paper, or leave dirty fragments all over your work. A soft putty eraser works best, since it absorbs pencil lead rather than just rubbing it away. For this reason, putty erasers do become dirty with use. Keep yours clean by trimming it carefully with scissors every now and then.

INKING PENS

The range of inking pens can be bewildering, but some basic rules will help you select the pens you need. Inked lines in most types of manga tend to be quite bold so buy a thin nibbed pen, about 0.5mm, and a medium-size nib, about 0.8mm. Make sure that the ink in the pens is waterproof; this won't smudge or run. Next, you will need a medium-tip felt pen. Although you won't need to use this pen very often to ink the outlines of your characters, it is still useful for filling in small detailed areas of solid black. A Pentel pen does this job well. Last, consider a pen that can create different line widths according to the amount of pressure you put on the tip. These pens replicate brushes and allow you to create flowing lines such as those seen on hair and clothing. The Pentel brush pen does this very well, delivering a steady supply of ink to the tip from a replaceable cartridge. It is a good idea to test-drive a few pens at your art shop to see which ones suit you best. All pens should produce clean, sharp lines with a deep black pigment.

Markers come in a wide variety of colours, which allows you to achieve subtle variations in tone. In addition to a thick nib for broad areas of colour, the Copic markers shown here feature a thin nib for fine detail.

A selection of warm and cool greys is a useful addition to your marker colours and most ranges feature several different shades. These are ideal for shading on faces, hair, and clothes.

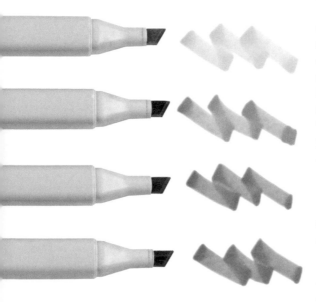

MARKERS AND COLOURING AIDS

Many artists use markers, rather than paint, to colour their artwork, because markers are easy to use and come in a huge variety of colours and shades. Good-quality markers, such as those made by Chartpak, Letraset or Copic, produce excellent, vibrant results, allowing you to build up multiple layers of colour so you can create rich, detailed work and precise areas of shading. Make sure that you use your markers with marker or layout paper to avoid bleeding. Markers are often refillable, so they last a long time. The downside is that they are expensive,

so choose a limited number of colours to start with, and add as your needs evolve. As always, test out a few markers in your art store before buying any.

However, markers are not the only colouring media. Paints and gouache also produce excellent results, and can give your work a distinctive look. Add white gouache, which comes in a tube, to your work to create highlights and sparkles of light. Apply it in small quantities with a good-quality watercolour brush. It is also possible to colour your artwork on computer. This is quick to do, although obviously there is a high initial outlay. It also tends to produce flatter colour than markers or paints.

DRAWING AIDS

Most of your sketching will be done freehand, but there are situations, especially with man-made objects such as the edges of buildings or the wheels of a car, when your line work needs to be crisp and sharp to create the right look.

If you are colouring with gouache or watercolour paint, then a selection of sizes of good quality sable watercolour brushes are invaluable.

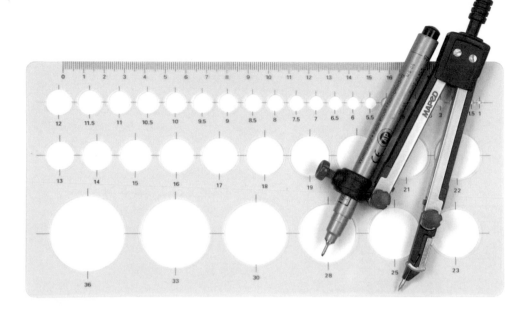

Rulers, circle guides and compasses all provide this accuracy. Rulers are either metal or plastic; in most cases, plastic ones work best, though metal ones tend to last longer. For circles, use a circle guide, which is a plastic sheet with a wide variety of different-sized holes stamped out of it. If the circle you want to draw is too big for the circle guide, use a compass that can hold a pencil and inking pen.

If you want to draw manga comic strips, a pencil and a standard 30cm (12in) ruler are the only tools you will need to plan out your panels. (It is also possible to draw them digitally on computer.) Just remember to buy a quality ruler with an edge that will suit your pencils and pens and won't chip over time. A plastic one will generally last longer than a wooden one. Creating speech bubbles inside the panels is best done by hand, but templates are available if you need help. They do make your work look neat, they are generally cheap to buy, and they

Working freehand allows great freedom of expression and is ideal when you are working out a sketch, but you will find times when precision is necessary. Use compasses or a circle guide for circles and ellipses to keep your work sharp. Choose compasses that can be adjusted to hold both pencils and pens.

do not need replacing often. You can buy them in most art shops. It is possible to order authentic manga templates from Japan, but these are not really necessary unless you want to start collecting authentic manga art equipment. You can make your own templates out of cardboard if the ones in the shops do not suit your needs.

DRAWING BOARD

A drawing board is useful, since working on a flat table for a long time can give you a backache. Lots of different models are available, but all should be adjustable to the angle at which you want to work. They also come in a wide variety of sizes, from ones that sit on your lap or a tabletop to large work tables. If you do not want to invest in one immediately, it is possible to prop a piece of smooth, flat plywood about 60cm (24in) x 45cm (18in) on your desk. Put a small box underneath to create an angled surface.

A mannequin can be placed in different poses, helping you to visualise action and movement.

MANNEQUIN

A mannequin is an excellent tool for helping you to establish correct anatomical proportions, particularly for simpler poses such as walking and running. All the limbs are jointed to mimic human movement. They are also relatively cheap, but bear in mind that other reference materials may be necessary for more complicated movements, such as those involving martial arts. Photographic reference is often useful too.

USING A COMPUTER

When your sketches start coming easily and the more difficult features, such as texture and perspective, begin to look more convincing, you will be confident enough to expand on the range of scenes you draw. You might even begin to compose cartoon strips of your own or, at the very least, draw compositions in which several characters interact with each other – such as a battle scene.

Once you reach this stage, you might find it useful to start using a computer alongside your regular art materials. Used with a software program, like Adobe Photoshop, you can colour scanned-in sketches quickly and easily. You will also have a much wider range of colours to use, and can experiment at will. Moving one step further, a computer can save you a lot of time and energy when it comes to producing comic strips. Most software programs enable you to build a picture in layers. This means that you could have a general background layer – say a mountainous landscape – that always stays the same, plus a number of subsequent layers on

Once you have scanned your line artwork you can use computer programs, such as Adobe Photoshop, to colour your drawings and add some original material as well. The choice is a matter of personal preference. The speed of a computer makes adding colour to manga easy, once you have learnt the process.

which you can build your story. For example, you could use one layer for activity that takes place in the sky and another layer for activity that takes place on the ground. This means that you can create numerous frames simply by making changes to one layer, while leaving the others as they are. There is still a lot of work involved, but working this way does save you from having to draw the entire frame from scratch each time.

Of course, following this path means that you must invest in a computer if you don't already have one. You will also need a scanner and the relevant software. All of this can be expensive and it is worth getting your hand drawn sketches up to a fairly accomplished level before investing too much money.

You can input a drawing straight into a computer program by using a graphics tablet and pen. The tablet plugs into your computer, much like a keyboard or mouse.

FACES AND AGE

All faces begin with the same very basic oval shape, divided vertically and horizontally into four sections. These guides make it easier to position the facial features. You can adapt the shape of the basic oval depending on the age and gender of your character.

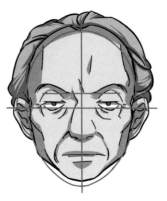

A child's face is, on the whole, shorter and rounder than that of an adult. In manga art, the eyes of a child are more exaggerated – almost as tall as they are wide.

In young adults, the face fills the oval guide more fully. Eyes are slimmer and tend to be more realistic in appearance. Adult men have a strong jaw line.

This drawing shows typical features of an older manga male. The hairline has receded, the eyelids are heavy, and the jaw line has more definition.

A similar oval shape is used for drawing side profiles. Childlike features are simple, with the emphasis on the large eyes.

This adult male has a sharper profile than the boy. His face is longer, the chin more pointed, and his nose is better defined.

Older manga characters are often more realistic. This man has a rounded nose and chin and small, deep-set eyes.

THREE-QUARTER VIEW

Drawing a face from the three-quarter view also works using an oval guideline, but this time it is slightly tilted. The important thing here is to draw the vertical guide (with a slight curve at the forehead) one-third of the way across the face. This will help to get the perspective right.

The large eyes of the manga boy are wide set. The light is coming from the left, so any shading needs to be on the right.

When drawing the adult male from this angle, it is important to capture the squarer lines of the jawbone.

The heavy lines of the older manga man give an impression of the bone structure beneath the skin. The forehead is exposed.

FACES AND ANGLES

You can draw a face from any angle, but it is important to get the proportions and perspective right. Start with a basic oval each time and consider where the vertical and horizontal guidelines might need to be in order to help you get it right.

A three-quarter view looking upwards. The vertical guide should be one-third in from the left, with the horizontal guide drawn as an upward curve.

This is a straightforward three-quarter view.

A three-quarter view looking down. The horizontal guide should be drawn as a downward-facing curve.

A side view looking up. The vertical guide is central, while the horizontal guide should tilt from bottom left to top right.

The guides for a side view are the same as those face on. Here, the vertical guide helps to position the ear.

This character is seen slightly from above and there is slight foreshortening of the face.

FACE SHAPES

Most manga characters are lean and youthful. Younger faces tend to be fuller and older faces more human looking. In all cases, characteristics can be exaggerated to make the shape of the face more in keeping with the intended personality.

left The fuller face of a young character. His facial features are tiny, exaggerating the roundness of his cheeks. He has a wide neck and smooth jaw line. He does not look threatening or harmful in any way.

right This is the face of a more mature adult male, with hollow cheeks and a pointed chin. All of his facial features are narrow, the eyes and eyebrows slanting upwards.

left The character on the left has a more rugged appearance, achieved by giving him a much squarer face. His eyes are deeper set and he has a firmer jaw line.

MAN'S FACE SIDE VIEW

You can follow these steps to draw any face side on. This example shows a young man. He has sharp masculine features, and is quite human looking. Adapt the shape of the face to suit any character you like, changing facial features accordingly.

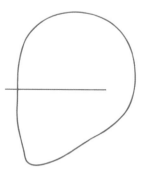

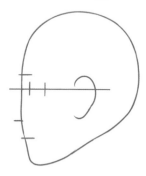

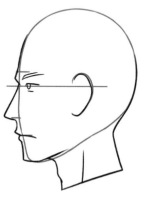

Start with a pencil outline of a tapered oval, tipped slightly to one side. Mark the centre line on the horizontal axis.

Divide the profile of the oval into thirds and mark the position of the eye on the horizontal guide, a little way in from the edge.

Draw in basic features. The eyebrow should sit on the top-third horizontal guide. Give shape to the nose and neck.

Draw in an outline for the hair, making it stand **proud of** the oval guide for an impression of volume. Add detail to the ear.

Go over your drawing in ink, adding more detail to the eye and giving more texture to the hair here and there.

Colour your work, paying close attention to the direction of the light. Use flat colour before working on the shaded areas.

MAN'S FACE LOOKING UP

This face is drawn from a three-quarter view. Although the horizontal guide remains halfway down the face, it should have an upward curve to it. This will help to position the eyes correctly.

 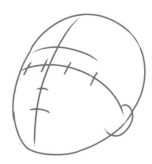 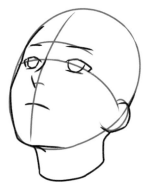

Draw a basic oval, tapered and tilted back slightly. Draw in the vertical and horizontal guides as described above.

Divide the face into equal thirds horizontally and into fifths vertically. Allow for perspective as you do so.

Position the facial features. Notice how the ears are lower than the eyes and not level with them, as in the previous faces.

Draw in an outline for the hair. Make it stand proud of the oval guide at the top and back to aid perspective. Add detail to the ear.

Go over your drawing in ink, adding more detail to the eyes and giving more texture to the hair in places.

Colour your work, paying close attention to the direction of the light. Use flat colour before working on the shaded areas.

EYE STYLES

The eyes are almost always the most important facial feature in manga art. Very often they are exaggerated in size and shape and dominate the face. You can use size, shape and colour to great effect when building on the personality of a character.

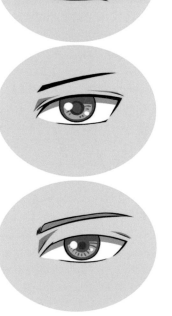

Children: Eyes are at their biggest in manga children, almost as tall as they are wide and with huge pupils. Boys' eyes are more angular than girls'.

Teenagers: Although smaller than those of children, teenage eyes are still exaggerated.

Young adult: Mature manga characters tend to have more realistic eyes.

Older adult: There is more shaping to the eye socket in the older manga and a change in eyebrow colour. Notice how much smaller the pupil is.

DRAWING EYES

These are the two sorts of eye you are likely to use most – the larger-than-life youth's eye and the half-realistic adult eye. You can use these models to draw eyes for all your characters; just remember to keep female eyes more rounded and male eyes more angular.

SLIM MALE EYES

Begin with a partial outline, keeping the shape long and thin, with slight angles at the corners. Draw a part-obscured iris.

Draw in the eyebrow, making sure it echoes the shape and angularity of the eye. Add lines to suggest the eye socket.

Go over your work in ink and colour the image. Shade the eye where the lid casts a shadow and add bright highlights.

NOSE STYLES

There are several different styles to choose from when it comes to giving your manga character a nose. They range from a single line to mark the bottom of the nose, to the full-blown, human-style variety. You need to consider perspective carefully.

Drawing just the curve at the bottom of the nose is a simple option. Adding nostrils (left) is also an option. These are typically used for children.

Teenage noses tend to have a more angular quality, drawn using very simple lines (right). Casting a shadow to one side (left) helps define the shape.

Adult noses are more realistic in appearance. The shapes are drawn more fully. These types of noses work better when drawn with nostrils.

The noses of older manga characters are the most realistic of all. They can be smooth (left) or bony and gnarled (right).

EAR STYLES

When it comes to drawing ears, there are variations for a range of ages and scope for adapting them to suit any character you like. Of all the facial features in manga art, the ears tend to look the most realistic and you need to be able to draw them from a variety of different angles.

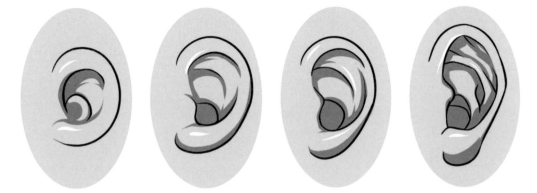

left to right The simplest style of ear is that of the chibi – the youngest character. The ear is almost round and has very little detail. In older children the ear is still simple, though longer. Young adults have more realistic ears, elongated in shape and with more detail. For the older manga characters a wholly realistic ear works well. This tends to have more shape and detail.

EARS AND ANGLES

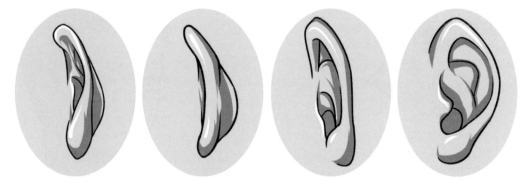

left to right Capturing the appearance of an ear accurately can be very difficult. They are awkward shapes and complex to draw from certain angles. You need to take perspective into account, which often involves foreshortening. These examples show the ear drawn variously from behind, a three-quarter view and side on. Notice how shape and visibility change.

MALE SHORT HAIR

Hair doesn't get much shorter than this! The short crop is a neat haircut, almost always used for male characters. Note how the line of the hair follows the oval guideline very closely, and sits on the dotted hairline across the forehead.

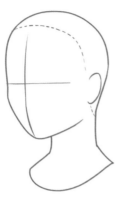

Begin with a pencil outline of the man's head, seen from the three-quarter view. Draw in your basic guidelines.

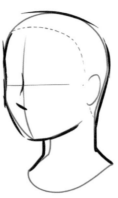

Give more shape to the face. Draw in a simple nose and square off the chin. Start the outline for the hair.

The hair should sit on the hairline, but stand proud of the oval guide for the man's profile. Draw in the facial features.

Firm up the outline of the hair, adding a few lines to suggest texture. Draw the eyes in greater detail. Add some eyebrows.

Finish the eyebrows and give shape to the neck. Go over your outline in ink. Erase unwanted pencil lines.

Add colour using flat tones before working on shadows and highlights. Pay attention to the direction of light.

BOY WITH SHORT SPIKY HAIR

This boy's hairstyle is very spiky. The character's facial features help to emphasize his look, with harsh, angular eyes.

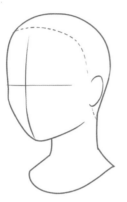

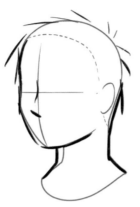

Draw your basic oval shape, with three-quarter view guidelines. Mark the hairline across the top of the head with a dotted line.

Draw a basic outline of the boy's profile and add rough lines to suggest the hair. See how these follow the curve of the head.

Use your guides to position the boy's facial features. Draw the outline of his spiky fringe, using sharp, straight lines.

Work on the outline of the boy's hair, making the spikes uneven for greater emphasis. Give him angular eyes and eyebrows.

Add any final details – the boy's collarbones, for example. Square up the jaw and finish the ear. Go over your drawing in ink.

Colour your artwork. The harsh features are emphasised by the cold hair colour. There is a strong contrast between light and dark.

SHORT CLEAN-CUT HAIR

This is a great hairstyle for a character who is in the service of an employer or some sort of organization. Soft and rounded, it is not a haircut that exudes power, despite the look of anger on the man's face. It would work well with a uniform.

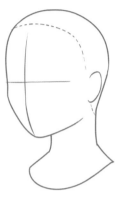

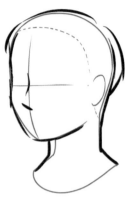

Draw your basic oval shape, with three-quarter view guidelines. Mark the hairline across the top of the head with a dotted line.

Draw a basic outline of the man's profile and add a smooth line for the hair. See how it follows the oval guide.

This man has a high fringe, drawn simply as a straight line across the forehead. Position the man's facial features.

Draw in the eyebrows. Like the man's hair, they are thick. Note how they rise at an angle, because the man is angry.

Draw any final details – inside the man's mouth, for example. Finish the ear and go over your artwork in ink.

Colour your image, considering the direction of light. The hair is thick and glossy. Use dark tones to pick out a few individual hairs.

MEDIUM-LENGTH HAIR

Medium-length hair tends to be about chin length. It can be straight or wavy. As **for** short hair, it helps to have the same guidelines that you use for drawing faces as well as a dotted guide for the hairline.

A boy with thick, soft, layered hair. There is more volume than you get with short spiky hair, and this is achieved by drawing the outline a little above the oval guide.

A boy with swept-back spiked hair. Note how the cut sits on the dotted hairline, but stands well above the oval guide. Although spiked, this remains a soft look.

BOY'S MESSY HAIR

This cut is a longer version of the spiked hair on page 30. The lines are softer and there is more volume. This, together with the warmer, more friendly facial features, particularly the large round eyes, give the boy a gentler appearance.

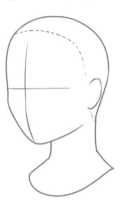

Draw your basic oval shape, with three-quarter view guidelines. Mark the hairline across the top of the head with a dotted line.

Draw a basic outline of the boy's profile and add sweeping lines to suggest the hair. They should sit on the oval guide.

Add the outline of his floppy fringe, using loose, curved lines. Use your guides to position the boy's facial features.

Work on the outline of the boy's hair, keeping it shaggy and uneven. Give him wide round eyes and arched eyebrows.

Finish the eyebrows and give shape to the neck. Go over your outline in ink. Erase unwanted pencil lines.

Colour your artwork, using flat colour before adding darker tones for shaded areas and a few subtle highlights.

COMBED-BACK HAIR

This style is swept back away from the face. It is a good style for the mature adult, as demonstrated here, but would also suit a young, sophisticated self-confident man.

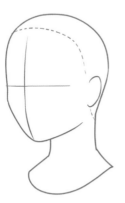

Draw your basic oval shape, with three-quarter view guidelines. Mark the hairline across the top of the head with a dotted line.

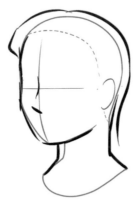

Draw in a basic outline of the man's profile and add strong lines to suggest the smooth sweep of the hair.

Position the man's facial features and add more lines to the hair. It should sit on or near the hairline guide, sweeping backwards.

Continue to work on the hair, keeping it neatly backswept. Finish the facial features, keeping them quite realistic.

Finish the eyes and ear and give more shape to the neck. Go over your outline in ink, and erase unwanted pencil lines.

Colour your artwork, using flat colour to start with. Work carefully to get a good mix of light and dark strands.

GALLERY

exaggerated spikes

above Based on the spiked haircut (right), this could be used for older boys and teenagers. The tresses at the sides are really exaggerated.

spikes all around

above Most suitable for the younger male characters, this kind of cut brings a certain unruly air to the character.

male student

above Long, lank and unstyled, this is definitely the look of a teenage boy — a student or band member, perhaps.

sweeping spikes

above This boy has long and thick spikes brushed forward from the crown. Notice how the shading mirrors the shapes of the spikes for maximum effect.

laid back

above This shows how a ponytail can be used successfully on a male character. As long as the hair is tied low, it will create the right laid-back look.

raven-like

above Both the colouring and styling of this cut would suit a half-man, half-bird character: the close cropping is reminiscent of a bird's feathers.

trendsetter

above Both the style and the colouring suggest someone who is avant-garde. The deep fringe partially obscures the face, while the ponytail is short and spiked.

sweeping spikes

above The hair is brushed towards the centre line all the way from front to back. It would suit a youthful character.

innocence

above This simple, rounded hairstyle betrays a certain innocence in the character. This is emphasised by the soft, muted colouring.

mature

above Neat and sophisticated, this swept-back look is the preserve of the more mature adult male.

BODY COMPARISONS

Compare the male and female versions of the manga characters depicted on these pages. You will see straight away that the male versions tend to be a little taller than their female counterparts, yet there are a good number of similarities to take note of, too.

below
The elderly. In terms of proportion, older characters tend to divide into fifths. The head makes up one-fifth, the torso two-fifths and the legs two-fifths. The shapes of their bodies are not as well-defined as in younger characters, and they wear loose-fitting clothes.

above
The mature adult. Body proportions work on sevenths, here, where the head is one-seventh, the torso roughly two-and-a-half, and the legs roughly three-and-a-half. Figures are lean and muscled in men and more shapely in women.

above

Chibis. Physically, there are no differences between male and female chibis – this has to come down to hair and clothing. Proportionally, their heads make up one-third of their body size.

above

Teenagers. Differences between male and female characters begin to emerge as they enter their teenage years. Boys are a little taller and more muscular than girls, while girls are slimmer with natural curves and well-defined waistlines. Facial features in girls tend to be softer. Proportions are the same as for the mature adult.

right

Manga children. Boys and girls are almost identical and usually only distinguishable by their clothing and hairstyles. Boys tend to have less shapely limbs and thicker necks. Proportions are the same as for the elderly

BODY TYPES

In manga art, characters are almost always healthy looking. Even if they are not youthful, their bodies tend to be in good shape. For the purposes of this book, we have selected three body types. There are obviously many variations, but these offer a good starting point.

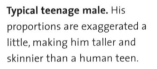
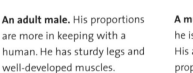

Typical teenage male. His proportions are exaggerated a little, making him taller and skinnier than a human teen.

An adult male. His proportions are more in keeping with a human. He has sturdy legs and well-developed muscles.

A muscled adult male. Super fit he is a power house of strength. His anatomy is still well-proportioned.

SIMPLE ANATOMY

The body can be drawn as a series of simple geometric shapes. Use ovals or circles for the head and joints. Working in this way, you'll soon start to see the relationship between different parts of the body and how these change with movement.

right Seated figure, seen from a three-quarter view. The challenge here is to keep the foreshortened thighs in proportion.

below A dancing figure. All of the limbs are stretched with the movement, as the figure clearly balances on tiptoe.

above A standing figure, arms by the side. Note how the body is slightly turned to one side, with one leg stepping forward.

above An athletic leaping or running figure. You can see how the arms and legs are working together to pull forward.

MALE STANDING

This man is standing in a relaxed pose. His feet are roughly hip-width apart and his arms hang loosely by his sides. The steps below can be used for any character of any age and gender. You may have to adjust the proportions slightly.

Build on your structure using simple geometric shapes to draw the body parts. Use ovals or circles to link your shapes together at the joints.

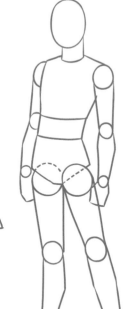

Draw in the man's eyes and an outline of his hair. Start to define his skeletal structure, drawing in details like the collarbone, pelvis and kneecaps.

Sketch a very rough structure of your man using a pencil. Think carefully about the proportions. The hands should reach the mid-thigh area.

Use your structural work to draw a solid outline. Think about his muscular make-up. Draw in guides for positioning the man's facial features.

Once you are happy with your pencil drawing, go over just the outline of the man's body in ink.

Now you can add colour to your drawing. It is important to consider the direction from which the light is coming. This will help you to decide where the shaded areas are.

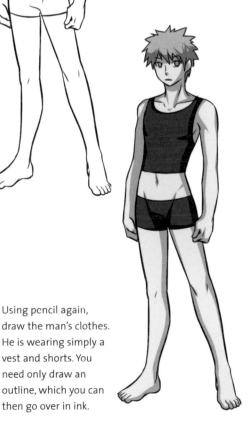

Work on the upper body now. Draw in the man's chest and round his shoulders a little. Give more shape to the arms and hands.

Using pencil again, draw the man's clothes. He is wearing simply a vest and shorts. You need only draw an outline, which you can then go over in ink.

RUNNING BOY

The key to getting this character right is being able to capture the movement of his running. You need to understand how the limbs work together in order to drive the body forward. It might help to have a few photographic references as guides.

Draw geometric shapes for the body parts, linking them together at the joints with circles or ovals. You need to think about body shape and perspective.

Really work on the positions of the boy's limbs. You need to think about the effects of foreshortening in order to draw them accurately.

Start with a basic pencil structure, paying particular attention to the positions of the arms and legs.

Use your basic structure to draw a solid outline. Make the boy more athletic in appearance. Draw in guides for the hair and facial features.

Once you are happy with your pencil drawing, go over just the outline of the boy's body in ink. Take care to follow your sketch faithfully.

Now you can add colour to your drawing. Use flat colour to start with. You can then build on the areas of light and shade. Take care not to lose the muscular physique beneath the Lycra clothing.

Build on the athletic shape of the boy's body. Make his arms and chest more muscular and round off the bent knee.

Use a pencil to draw the boy's clothes. He is wearing an all-in-one. You need only draw an outline, which you can then go over in ink.

BOY JUMPING

This is a very dramatic pose, bursting with movement and energy. The boy is young and you need to be able to demonstrate this, capturing the agility of his limbs as he moves. This pose would suit a number of characters.

Build on your structure using simple geometric shapes to draw the body parts. Use ovals or circles to link your shapes together at the joints.

Keep your lines smooth to help capture the motion. Try to draw a continuous line from the top of the upraised hand to the tip of the near foot.

Start with your basic pencil structure, thinking carefully about body shape as well as proportions, and that every part of his body is in motion.

Use your structural work to draw a solid outline. Think about the tension in the limbs as the boy is suspended in the air. Draw in guides for the hair and facial features.

Once you are happy with your pencil drawing, go over just the outline of the boy's body in ink. Remember to keep your lines smooth and sweeping.

Colour your drawing. Use flat colours to start with, after which you can build on the areas of light and shade.

Build on the boy's skeletal and muscular structure, particularly around the shoulder area and ribcage.

Use a pencil to draw the boy's T-shirt and shorts. Note how the bottom of the shirt is lifted by the force of the motion. Try to capture this.

47

MAN PLAYING FOOTBALL

This pose is all about the action of kicking a football, with the character still in motion as he watches the ball pound into the back of the net. You need to judge the positions of the limbs carefully in order to capture the movement.

Start with your basic pencil structure, thinking carefully about body shape as well as proportion, and that the man is balancing on just one leg.

Build on your structure using simple geometric shapes to draw the body parts. Use ovals or circles to link your shapes together at the joints.

Use your structural work to draw a solid outline. Think about the tension in the limbs as they keep balance. Draw in guides for the hair and facial features.

Review your outline. You really need to capture the tension in the limbs.

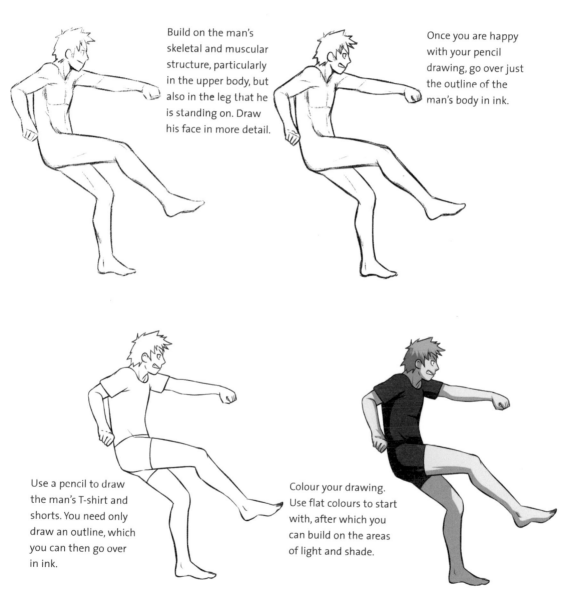

Build on the man's skeletal and muscular structure, particularly in the upper body, but also in the leg that he is standing on. Draw his face in more detail.

Once you are happy with your pencil drawing, go over just the outline of the man's body in ink.

Use a pencil to draw the man's T-shirt and shorts. You need only draw an outline, which you can then go over in ink.

Colour your drawing. Use flat colours to start with, after which you can build on the areas of light and shade.

BOY SITTING ON FLOOR

This is a very comfortable pose, seated cross-legged on the floor, and with the arms resting gently on the knees. A suitable pose for both genders.

Use a pencil to sketch a basic structure. The back is rigid and upright and both legs are crossed in front of the boy.

Use simple geometric shapes to draw the body parts, linking them together at the joints with circles or ovals. Think about perspective.

Use this structure to draw a solid outline. Think about the boy's muscular make-up as you do this. Draw in the guides for hair and facial features.

Give more shape to the boy's body, drawing his arms and legs more accurately.

Work on the abdomen now, adding feint lines to define his muscles. Draw in facial features and the boy's fingers.

Once you are happy with your pencil drawing, go over just the outline of the boy's body in ink. Take care to follow your sketch accurately.

Use a pencil to draw the boy's clothes. He is wearing a vest and shorts. You need only draw an outline, which you can then go over in ink.

Add colour. Use flat colour to start with, then build on the areas of light and shade. Do not lose the muscular physique beneath the Lycra clothing.

Chapter Five

Men's Manga Clothing

CLOTHING

Search through books or the Internet for examples of traditional costumes from across the world. Japanese kimonos, Spanish flamenco dresses and Indian saris can all form the basis of a character's outfit, as shown with the female character below.

The straightforward suit is a very versatile outfit and can be adapted for a wide range of characters from professional male to evil schemer.

Think of the many careers that involve the wearing of a uniform from hotel staff, to firefighters and elaborate on them to make your own designs.

DRAWING CREASES

Almost all clothing will have folds or creases. The only exceptions are Lycra and metal plate and, even then, you may have the odd wrinkle or riveted seam! Folds tend to be more evident, often deeper, in the lighter-weight fabrics, such as cotton and silk.

Shirt collars and the tops of jumpers follow the natural curves of the neck and shoulder line. They crease where the straight fabric is forced to bend.

Softer fabrics will always crease in areas that are looser-hanging than others, like this hood. Here the pull is from the shoulders and down the centre of the back.

Trousers hang vertically from the knee and are looser around the foot area. Creases form where the material bunches.

GALLERY

Being able to draw clothes accurately is key to creating realistic-looking manga characters. It is important to consider the weight and texture of the fabric and the body shape of the wearer. The way in which the fabric has been used or is being worn is also significant.

windswept jacket

right This character is riding a bike. See how his jacket flaps about, making numerous flowing folds as the fabric is caught by movement.

hand in pocket

above A hand in a pocket often makes the pocket area stretch. Creases around the pocket help to emphasise this.

bent joints

below Creases always radiate from the centre of a bent elbow or knee, no matter what fabric.

rolled sleeves

below All fabrics form loose bands when rolled or pushed up. Generally, the stiffer the fabric, the sharper the creases.

cotton T-shirt

above Cotton fabrics want to hang in a given direction and will crease when forced to hang differently – around arms and necks, for example.

BASEBALL CAP

The baseball cap is a wardrobe staple for boys and young men, although it may also be worn by girls. You can adapt the steps to draw the hat worn back to front.

Use pencil to draw your basic oval shape, with three-quarter view guidelines. Draw in your character's facial features.

Sketch in an outline of the cap and hair. Note how the cap follows the oval guide closely and extends out over the eyes.

Draw in the stitching lines on the cap. This will help to make the image look three-dimensional. Draw in the neck and ear.

 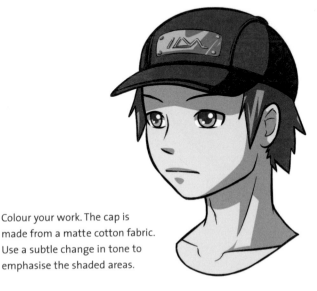

Add any final details, such as the badge on the cap and the shaping to the boy's neck. Go over your artwork in ink.

Colour your work. The cap is made from a matte cotton fabric. Use a subtle change in tone to emphasise the shaded areas.

BACKPACK

The trusty backpack is a manga favourite, used by young and old alike. Although this version is practical and compact, you can use the steps to design any backpack you like, from a fun and fluffy animal-shaped one for kids to the heavy-duty sort used by the military.

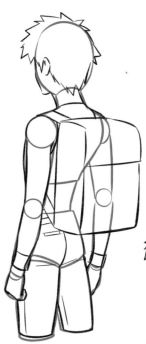

Start by drawing a pencil outline of your figure using basic geometric shapes. This man is viewed from the rear. Build on your outline to sketch the man and backpack more fully.

Add any final details – a little more texture in the hair, fine stitching on the backpack, creases in the clothing – before going over your artwork in ink.

Consider the size of the backpack and make sure it fits your characters proportions. Work on the details, drawing in the many pockets and straps.

Colour your work using appropriate shades. Use subtle tones to capture the changes from light to dark.

NINJA

Ninjas are extremely popular figures in manga art. Their characters are based on ancient Japanese warriors, whose activities were often clandestine. The clothing is mysterious, while the pose is very masterful.

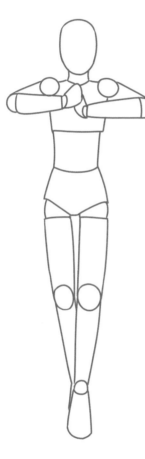

Use your outline as a guide for the clothing, keeping your lines simple. Draw in the protective leather shoulder pads.

Begin with a pencil outline using a series of geometric shapes. Give the man a stance in keeping with the nature of his character.

Give the character some hair and draw in the facial features. Begin to work more on the clothing, drawing in the metal plates on the sleeves.

Continue to add detail, bearing in mind the textures and weights of the various materials used. Draw in the long, sweeping scarf. Go over your work in ink.

Colour your work. Pay particular attention to the different materials and really try to capture the texture of the leather and metal elements.

Finish your drawing. There is a lot of detail here. Draw in the shoes and bound legs. Work creases into the lightweight fabric.

COURT SUIT

This is a Western-style outfit, associated with royal courts and the nobility of early 19th-century Europe. It is characterised by an elegant formality.

Use your outline as a guide for drawing the clothing. Use simple lines to achieve the basic shape of coat tails and breeches.

Finish the outline of the clothing and draw in the man's shoes.

Begin by drawing a pencil outline using simple geometric shapes. Give the man a formal stance in keeping with the style of the clothing.

Draw the rest of the coat and the man's stockinged legs and feet. Give the character some hair and draw in the facial features.

Erase any unwanted pencil lines before adding the last few details in ink.

Colour your work, using sombre tones to reflect the formality of the clothing. Use highlights to show where the luxuriant materials catch the light.

Start to add more detail. Draw in the outline of a cravat at the neck. Draw in some cuffs and buckles on the shoes. Go over your drawing in ink.

Add the decorative elements, such as the buttons on the shirt front and the trim of the jacket. Give more definition to the shoes.

ROCK MAN

This look is mostly associated with teenagers, and can be adapted for both boys and girls. You can have great fun with different hairstyles and colours. This young man has a dishevelled, punk-type haircut.

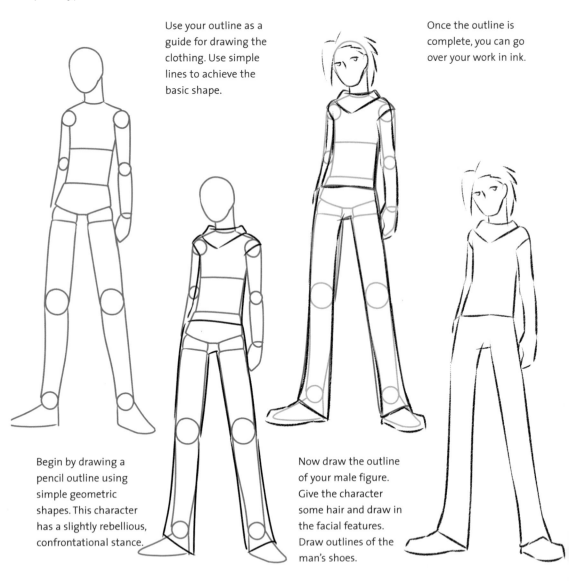

Use your outline as a guide for drawing the clothing. Use simple lines to achieve the basic shape.

Once the outline is complete, you can go over your work in ink.

Begin by drawing a pencil outline using simple geometric shapes. This character has a slightly rebellious, confrontational stance.

Now draw the outline of your male figure. Give the character some hair and draw in the facial features. Draw outlines of the man's shoes.

Erase your pencil lines in preparation for adding the finer ink details and colour.

Colour your work using strong colours. The soft shadows are almost black. Add a few subtle highlights where certain materials catch the light.

Draw in the loose belt around the man's waist and the straps on his trousers. Mark a few creases in the clothes. Draw shoes.

Add any final ink details, such as the stripes on the T-shirt and the decorative details on the man's armband, trousers, and shoes.

HIP-HOP BOY

This is a great look for the streetwise teenager – the slouchy hoodie and flared jeans of the hip-hop generation. You can easily adapt the clothes for a female character, but the look is best used for young adults and not older ones.

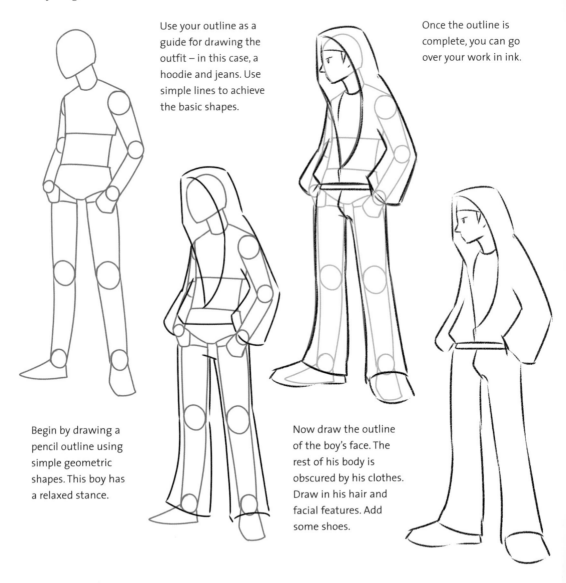

Use your outline as a guide for drawing the outfit – in this case, a hoodie and jeans. Use simple lines to achieve the basic shapes.

Once the outline is complete, you can go over your work in ink.

Begin by drawing a pencil outline using simple geometric shapes. This boy has a relaxed stance.

Now draw the outline of the boy's face. The rest of his body is obscured by his clothes. Draw in his hair and facial features. Add some shoes.

Erase your pencil lines in preparation for adding the finer ink details and colour.

Colour your work using low-key colours. Use darker tones to emphasise the creases in the fabric.

Add more detail. Draw in the boy's medallion and finish the shoes. Use a few feint lines to mark creases in the T-shirt, hoodie and jeans.

Add any final ink details, such as the flame motif on the hoodie and the stars on the boy's bandana.

SHORT HAIR BASICS

Many of your male characters will have short hair. The key to getting the look right is to follow the basic shape of your oval guide. Drawing a dotted hairline across the skull will help to get a realistic fringe and a more three-dimensional appearance.

left This boy has spiky hair, made by drawing short, jagged lines all the way around the oval guide. The texture of the hair is achieved through clever shading.

right Here is the same boy with straight hair. See how it hugs the oval guide at the crown and back of the neck. The fringe sweeps forward and across the forehead.

POLICEMAN

Police uniforms differ from country to country, so there are plenty of examples to base your designs on. You can also adapt this outfit to suit a wider range of uniforms, for example, for a military character, a park keeper or a hotel valet.

Using your pencil guide, sketch in the man's uniform. This example has a belted jacket and a peaked cap.

Once the outline is complete, you can go over your work in ink.

Begin by drawing a pencil outline using simple geometric shapes. This man is standing to attention.

Now draw the man's head and hands. Then draw his hair and facial features. Add outlines for his boots.

Erase your pencil lines in preparation for adding the finer ink details and colour.

Colour your work, using a flat, dark colour. The shadows in the creases will be black. Use highlights to show where the uniform catches the light.

Work on the finer details now – the creases in the man's jacket and trousers, the badge on his arm and the belt across his chest Finish the boots.

Add any final ink details, such as the buttons on his jacket, seams on his gloves and pouch on his belt.

GALLERY

When it comes to designing clothing, you can really use your imagination to draw a huge range of outfits. And there is no lack of source material. Just take a look at native costumes from around the world or the latest fashions and you will be inspired.

woodland boy

right The basic cut of the clothes and their earthy colours are fitting for a simple life in a small woodland or rural community.

streetwise

below The urban fashionista. Note the high collar and deep cuffs of the shirt with the double belt worn over the top.

futuristic

right The practical yet other-worldly uniform of a spaceship crew member, complete with cape and elbow-length armbands.

medieval

right The outfit of a workhand at a medieval castle. It has simple lines and is worn with bound legs and handmade boots.

young pup

right A playful looking outfit. The T-shirt worn over the shirt and the massive boots worn with knee-length shorts give a certain mismatched look.

GALLERY

You can have tremendous fun working on clothing ideas for your characters. Think about suitable textures and colours, as these often determine whether or not an outfit is successful. Put some thought into appropriate accessories, too.

countryman

right The smart outfit of a member of a medieval land-owning family. The clothing is made from soft fabrics in natural colours.

operator

below The protective overall and gloves of a workshop employee. This outfit has a certain fantasy element to it.

smart suit

right A snappy single-breasted suit. The good quality of the matte black material lends the suit an elegance.

mechanic

right The protective jumpsuit of a car mechanic or factory operator. Highly practical, the zip-up outfit tucks into heavy boots.

waif

right A young man who has fallen on hard times in an outfit that he has fashioned from sacking. It is tattered and torn.

anatomy The structure of a living thing; also, the study of this structure.

asymmetrical Having parts that are unequal in shape or size; lacking symmetry.

avant-garde Radically new or original; cutting-edge.

chibi Small or undersized; in manga and anime, a childlike character that is drawn to be very small and cute.

confrontational Given to starting conflict; aggressive.

cravat A wide band of fabric worn around the neck as a tie.

fashionista A person who follows trends in the fashion industry and continually strives to adopt the latest fashions.

flat color Color that has a single hue and value throughout.

foreshortening The technique of reducing or distorting parts of an object in a drawing in order to create an illusion of depth.

freehand Done by hand without mechanical aids or instruments (such as rulers).

gouache A water-based paint that is heavier and more opaque than watercolor.

mannequin An artist's jointed figure of the human body.

matte Having a dull finish without any shine or gloss.

obscure To conceal or hide by covering.

perspective The technique of representing three-dimensional objects on a two-dimensional surface, giving the illusion of depth and distance.

proportion The relationship in size of one part of a work of art to the whole, or to other parts (for example, the relationship of the head to the body).

shade To add lights and darks to a work of art, usually to create a three-dimensional effect.

shonen Young boy or boy; a generic term for manga and anime aimed at young males.

tapered Becoming gradually narrower toward one end.

torso The trunk of the human body.

Asian Art Museum
Chong-Moon Lee Center for Asian Art and
    Culture
200 Larkin Street
San Francisco, CA 94102
(415) 581-3500
Web site: http://www.asianart.org
The Asian Art Museum–Chong-Moon Lee Center
    for Asian Art and Culture is home to a world-
    renowned collection of more than eighteen
    thousand Asian art treasures. Through rich art
    experiences centered on historic and contemporary
    artworks, the museum unlocks the past for visitors,
    while serving as a catalyst for new art, new creativity,
    and new thinking.

Comic-Con International
P.O. Box 128458
San Diego, CA 92112-8458
(619) 491-2475
Web site: http://www.comic-con.org
Comic-Con International is a nonprofit educational
    organization dedicated to creating awareness of,
    and appreciation for, comics and related popular
    art forms, primarily through the presentation
    of conventions and events that celebrate the
    historic and ongoing contribution of comics to
    art and culture.

Japanese Canadian Cultural Centre (JCCC)
6 Garamond Court
Toronto, ON M3C 1Z5
Canada
(416) 441-2345
Web site: http://www.jccc.on.ca
Founded in 1963, the JCCC is one of the largest
and most vibrant Japanese cultural centers in the
world. It offers an array of Japanese traditional
and contemporary cultural programs, martial
arts, festivals, performances, film screenings, art
exhibitions, and other experiences for members
and visitors.

Japan Society
333 East 47th Street
New York, NY 10017
(212) 832-1155
Web site: http://www.japansociety.org
Japan Society is committed to deepening mutual
understanding between the United States and
Japan in a global context. The organization
provides a rich array of programs in arts and
culture, public policy, business, language, and
education for audiences of all ages.

Kyoto International Manga Museum
Karasuma-Oike

Nakagyo-ku
Kyoto 604-0846
Japan
Web site: http://www.kyotomm.jp/english
This museum acts as a venue for the collection,
    preservation, study, and exhibition of manga and
    animation materials. The museum holds a collection
    of approximately three hundred thousand items,
    including valuable historical materials and popular
    contemporary works from Japan and other
    countries.

Society for the Promotion of Japanese Animation
    (SPJA)
1733 S. Douglass Road, Suite F
Anaheim, CA 92806
(714) 937-2994
Web site: http://www.spja.org
This nonprofit organization aims to educate the
    American public about anime and manga, as well
    as provide a forum to facilitate communication
    between professionals and fans. The SPJA is the
    parent organization for Anime Expo, an anime and
    manga celebration held annually in Los Angeles.

Web Sites

Due to the changing nature of Internet links, Rosen
Publishing has developed an online list of Web sites related
to the subject of this book. This site is updated regularly.
Please use this link to access the list:

http://www.rosenlinks.com/MAMA/Men

Abel, Jessica, and Matt Madden. *Drawing Words & Writing Pictures: Making Comics: Manga, Graphic Novels, and Beyond.* New York, NY: First Second, 2008.

Antram, David. *Manga Action Figures* (How to Draw). New York, NY: PowerKids Press, 2012.

Antram, David. *Manga Warriors* (How to Draw). New York, NY: PowerKids Press, 2011.

Bigley, Al. *Draw Comics like a Pro: Techniques for Creating Dynamic Characters, Scenes, and Stories.* New York, NY: Watson-Guptill Publications, 2008.

Gray, Peter. *The Practical Guide to Drawing Manga* (Great Drawing Step-by-Step). New York, NY: Rosen Central, 2012.

Hart, Christopher. *Manga for the Beginner: Everything You Need to Know to Get Started Right Away!* New York, NY: Watson-Guptill Publications, 2008.

Hart, Christopher. *Young Artists Draw Manga.* New York, NY: Watson-Guptill Publications, 2011.

Ikari Studio, ed. *The Monster Book of Manga: Boys.* New York, NY: Collins Design, 2010.

Jones, Richard, and Jorge Santillan. *Manga Martial Arts Figures* (Learn to Draw Manga). New York, NY: PowerKids Press, 2013.

Jones, Richard, and Jorge Santillan. *Manga Superheroes* (Learn to Draw Manga). New York, NY: PowerKids Press, 2013.

Kallen, Stuart A. *Manga* (Eye on Art). Detroit, MI: Lucent Books, 2011.

Li, Yishan, and Andrew James. *Shonen Art Studio: Everything You Need to Create Your Own Shonen Manga Comics.* New York, NY: Watson-Guptill Publications, 2010.

Myo, Tamami. *How to Draw Manga: Drawing Bishonen*. Tokyo, Japan: Graphic-sha Publishing, 2008.

Okum, David. *Manga Martial Arts: Over 50 Basic Lessons for Drawing the World's Most Popular Fighting Styles*. Cincinnati, OH: Impact Books, 2008.

Orr, Tamra. *Manga Artists* (Extreme Careers). New York, NY: Rosen Publishing, 2009.

Singh, Asavari. *How to Draw the Most Exciting, Awesome Manga* (Velocity: Drawing). Mankato, MN: Capstone Press, 2012.

Southgate, Anna, and Keith Sparrow. *Drawing Manga Boys* (Manga Magic). New York, NY: Rosen Central, 2012.

INDEX

About the Authors

Anna Southgate is an experienced writer and editor who has worked extensively for publishers of adult illustrated reference books. Her recent work has included art instruction books and providing the text for a series of six manga titles.

Yishan Li is a professional manga artist living in Edinburgh, Scotland. Her work has been published in the UK, United States, France, and Switzerland. She has published many books on manga, and she also draws a monthly strip, *The Adventures of CGI*, for *CosmoGirl!*